KIDS PIANO!
MEMBERSHIP BOOK: LEVELS 11-13

This Book Belongs to:

Name:_____

Age:_____ Start Date:_____

Don't be a chicken! Play with both hands!

Don't be a Beethovatar! Play with both wings!

Table of Contents

A Rhymed History of How Music Came to Be

Our story begins around 500 B.C.

IT'S SUPER NEAT! READ IT AND SEE!

Heavy Metal!

Once upon a time, long ago in ancient Greece,
A guy named Pythagoras was walking the streets...

Some new CLING–CLANGING was very SWEET-SOUNDING...
Was it *blacksmiths*? Pounding *anvils*? Yes!
POUND-POUND-POUND-POUNDING!

CLANG?   TWANG?   KER-BANG!

BY ZEUS! THESE DUDES ROCK-OUT A SWEET MELODY!
HOW DO THESE ANVILS MAKE SUCH GREAT HARMONY?!

PYTHAGORAS

See, *these* anvils weren't ANY-old-anvils on shelves;
When *these* anvils were made, they were measured in 12^{ths}!

Upon inspecting the anvils, the thing that he found
Was that each of them made our 12 musical sounds!

BIG ONES rang LOW sounds, like HIPPOS on the ground! Small ones rang HIGH, like birds in the sky!

In fact, something neat that the Greeks liked to do
Was use their letters for NUMBERS, *and* MUSIC NOTES, too!

So if YOU time-traveled *waaaaay* back to ancient Greece,
You'd learn MATH, MUSIC, and READING with the *same* ABC's!

Did You Know...?

The numbers the Greeks used way back then
Repeated in 12's? (Not like us; We use 10!)

WHY 12 & not 10? Because 12, you see,
Is better for *CIRCLES*, like in *Geometry*!

Since it's in *CIRCLES* the earth & moon spin,
We count *HOURS* and *MONTHS* with 12, not 10!

"Why all the stuff about *CIRCLES?!*" you say?
Because of the body part that *hears* what we play...

Just a small way inside of your ear,
THIS is the organ that helps you to hear!
Which, the violin-makers MUST have been able to see,
Since it's the shape of the scroll *IDENTICALLY*!

So maybe, just *maybe*, our ears prefer SOUND
Divided in 12's because they're both ROUND!

Around 500 AD, Europe entered a stage
Known by historians as "The Dark Age."

Almost NO new songs were written or taught!
Songs played the past *THOUSAND YEARS* were *forgot*!

The Ancient Music Era had come to an end...
Making space for a NEW type of notes to begin!

THIRTEEN-HUNDRED YEARS BEFORE THE METRONOME, SONGS *STOPPED* BEING WRITTEN ACROSS MOST OF ROME!

500 years later (in 1013 AD),
Some-where-abouts in North Italy,
A choir-teaching *MONK* was in a musical *FUNK*...

I Wish I Could Write Down this Song in my **head**!
Or the World Will Forget it as Soon as I'm... **Asleep!**

He made the new notes in the time of Knights and Squires,
To be learned and performed by singers in choirs.

Unlike ancient Greeks, who wrote out each letter,
He thought "Just Dots on Lines are Better!"

But as time went by, instead of more *simplicity*,
His note system grew greater in **complexity**...

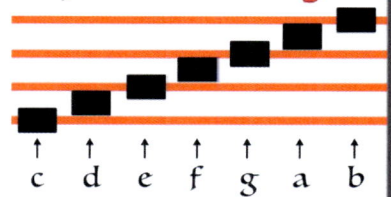

c d e f g a b

Each extra symbol became *more* and **more** CONFUSING,
Which made learning music *less* and **less** AMUSING!

But every so often, like once-in-a-*CENTURY*,
A *question* is asked that's quite *ELEMENTARY*!

Mr. Zach! WHAT IF notes were made JUST FOR *PIANO*?
If there wasn't SO MUCH that you needed to know?

What if, like those Greeks, we just *wrote out* each letter?
Could playing be *FUNNER?!* Would learning be *BETTER?!*

Mr. Bock! I think I have JUST what you seek!
To see how it works, turn the page! Have a peek!

1 The First Thing You Need to Know is How to Read *Beginner Notes!*

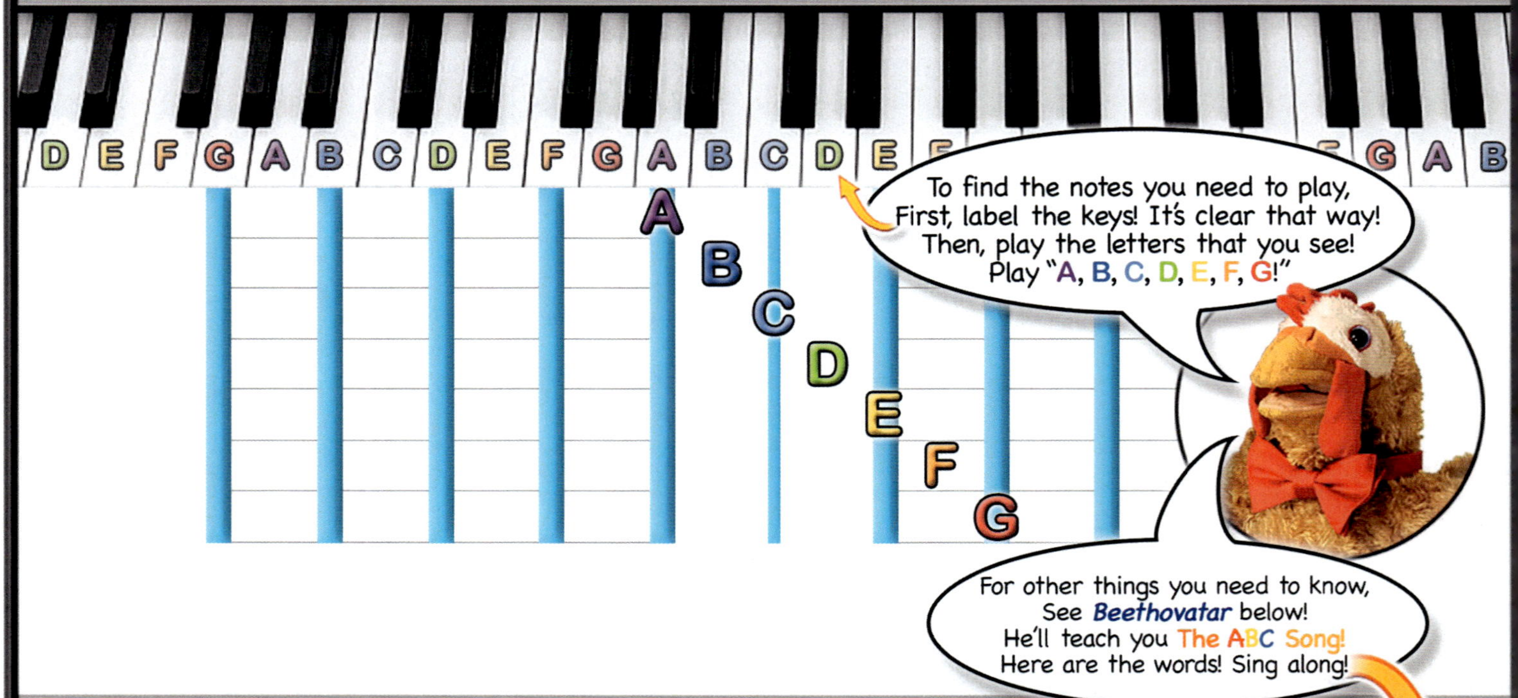

2

The 2nd Type of Innovation is *Intermediate Notation!*

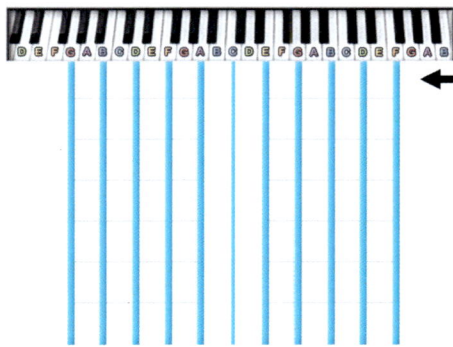

It's **Beginner Notes**, rotated *left*,
And given **Treble** 𝄞 and **Bass** 𝄢 clefs!

Read *these* notes from LEFT-to-RIGHT.
Here's *Middle C;*
Got it alright?

A B C D E F G

Hey! Now try Bach's *Prelude in C!*
Most people LOVE its melody!

Just *one last thing* before you do:
Left-hand is RED! Right-hand is BLUE!

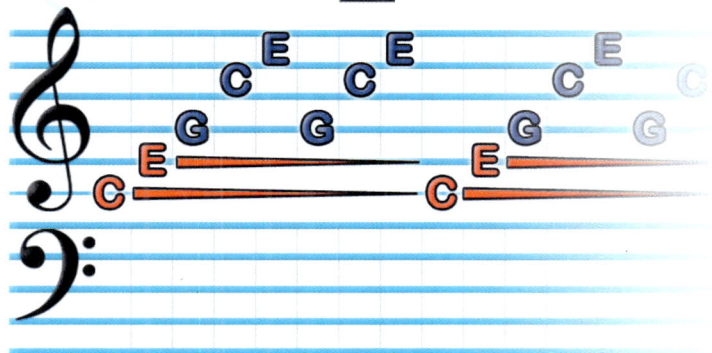

3

Exact-Notes' *Advanced Notes* Are Step #3 On Your Journey to Read Music *Traditionally!*

Use **Advanced Notes** for works *most debonair!*
Like Beethoven's *MOONLIGHT SONATA* and Bach's *WELL-TEMPERED CLAVIER!*

It's *quite* a special achievement to see
When kids get EXCITED to play songs like *these!*
Say, what's this here?! It's my *Fur Elise!*

"What is Bach's **Well-Tempered Clavier?**" did you say?
Oh, only how BEETHOVEN & MOZART learned to play!
It comes all the way back from *Old* Germany,
Bach's book, now for KIDS, from 1723!

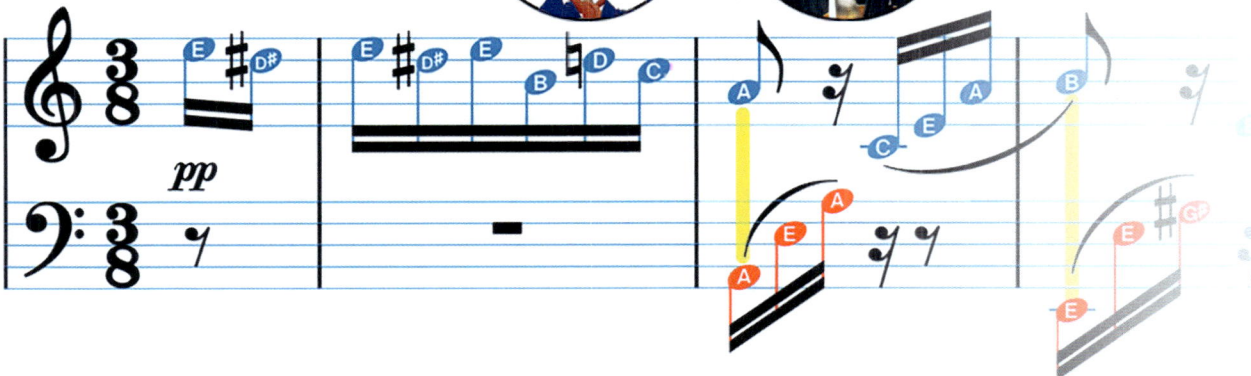

THE SYMBOLS OF MUSIC!

When playing Songs, RESTS don't mean to sleep! *(Zzz...?)*
In Music, they mean NOT to play for some beats!

EIGHTH RESTS look like 7's: they rest half-a-beat!

QUARTER RESTS rest for 1 beat: a *twice-as-long* sleep!

HALF RESTS look like *hat rests!* They rest for 2!

WHOLE RESTS get 4 beats! What a *snooze-a-paloo!!!*

THE REPEAT SIGN

If you see 2 dots at the end...
You have to play the song again!

CAN YOU SAY "*D.C. AL FINE?*"

Some words you'll see along the way
are pronounced "D.C. ahl fee-Nay!"

They work just like a repeat sign,
where "*Fine*" is the *Finish* line!

FERMATA

The FERMATA is the shape a conductor's hand makes
When showing *how long* a *long note* should take!

Their hand draws a circle, but when half-way around,
Closes into a fist (that's the "dot") to STOP all the sound!

DECELERANDO

If *slower* and *slower* and *slower* you go,
You are now playing "*DEH-CHEH-LEH-RAHN-DOH*"

You can remember it if all you know
is that "*DECELERATE*" means to "*GO SLOW!*"

ACCELERANDO

If *faster* and *faster* and *faster* you go,
you are now playing "*UH-CHEH-LEH-RAHN-DOH!*"

This is a word you will *QUICKLY* master
if you know "TO ACCELERATE" means "TO GO *FASTER!*"

NOW IT'S TIME FOR YOU TO SEE...
TREBLE & BASS CLEF HISTORY!

WHAT WAS THE TREBLE CLEF LIKE LONG, LONG AGO?
IT WAS A BIG "G" WITH A LONG UP-ARROW!
THE BIG DOT IS "MIDDLE C" AND IT POINTS TO HIGH G!
(IT SURE CHANGED A LOT AFTER 10 CENTURIES!)

BUT WHAT ABOUT THE OLD *BASS CLEF?*
THE *BASS CLEF* WAS A CURSIVE "F!"
WHAT'S THE BIG DOT MEAN ON THIS CLEF?
THE BIG DOT MEANS "THIS LINE PLAYS F!"

SHARPS #, NATURALS ♮, AND FLATS ♭

ARE SPECIAL SIGNS YOU WILL SEE IN MUSIC *THOUSANDS* OF TIMES!

#A #C #D #F #G   ♭A ♭B ♭D ♭E ♭G
  B   E   ♭C   ♭F

A B C D E F G A B C D E F G A B C D E F G

THE SHARP IS NOT STRAIGHT; NOT LIKE *TIC-TAC-TOE!*

+ ↗ =

IT SLANTS UP AND RIGHT
TO SHOW WHERE YOU GO!

THE NATURAL IS A NOTE THAT'S NOT SHARP *OR* FLAT!

♮ ♮ ♮ ♮ ♭

SEE HOW THE SIGNS MIX?
WELL, HOW ABOUT THAT?!

THE FLAT IS LIKE A DOWN ARROW, BUT HALF DOES NOT SHOW!

↓ ↓ ♭

IT TELLS YOU TO GO
LEFT (ONE KEY *BELOW*)!

SIGNS YOU SEE WHEN SONGS GET HARD
ARE DOUBLE FLATS ♭♭ AND *DOUBLE SHARPS* 𝄪!

BOTH OF THESE ARE *EXTREME* RARITIES, ONLY USED IN THE *MOST* ADVANCED KEYS!

WHEN YOU SEE A DOUBLE FLAT ♭♭,
GO TWO KEYS DOWN, OR TWO KEYS BACK,
WHETHER THEY ARE WHITE OR BLACK!

WHEN YOU SEE A DOUBLE SHARP 𝄪,
GO TWO KEYS UP, OR TWO KEYS RIGHT,
WHETHER THEY ARE BLACK OR WHITE!

THE DOUBLE SHARP, THOUGH, I KNOW YOU HAVE SEEN...
IT'S THE "X" IN E𝄪ACT-NOTES! *SEE WHAT I MEAN?!*

#34. HOT CROSS BUNS, *OUCH!*
Level 11: Songs in Parallel Motion

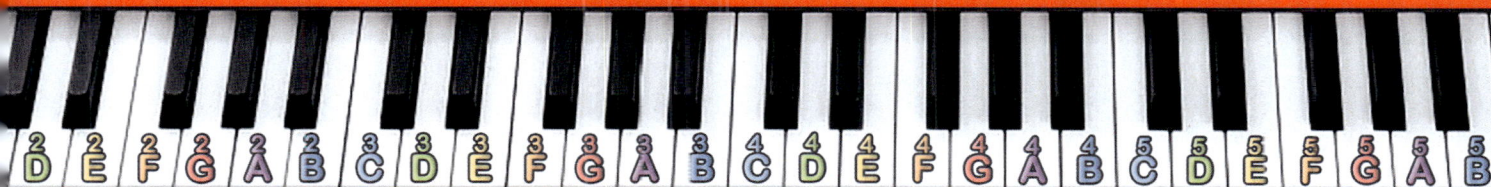

#35. MARY HAD A LITTLE LAMB!

Level 11: Songs in Parallel Motion

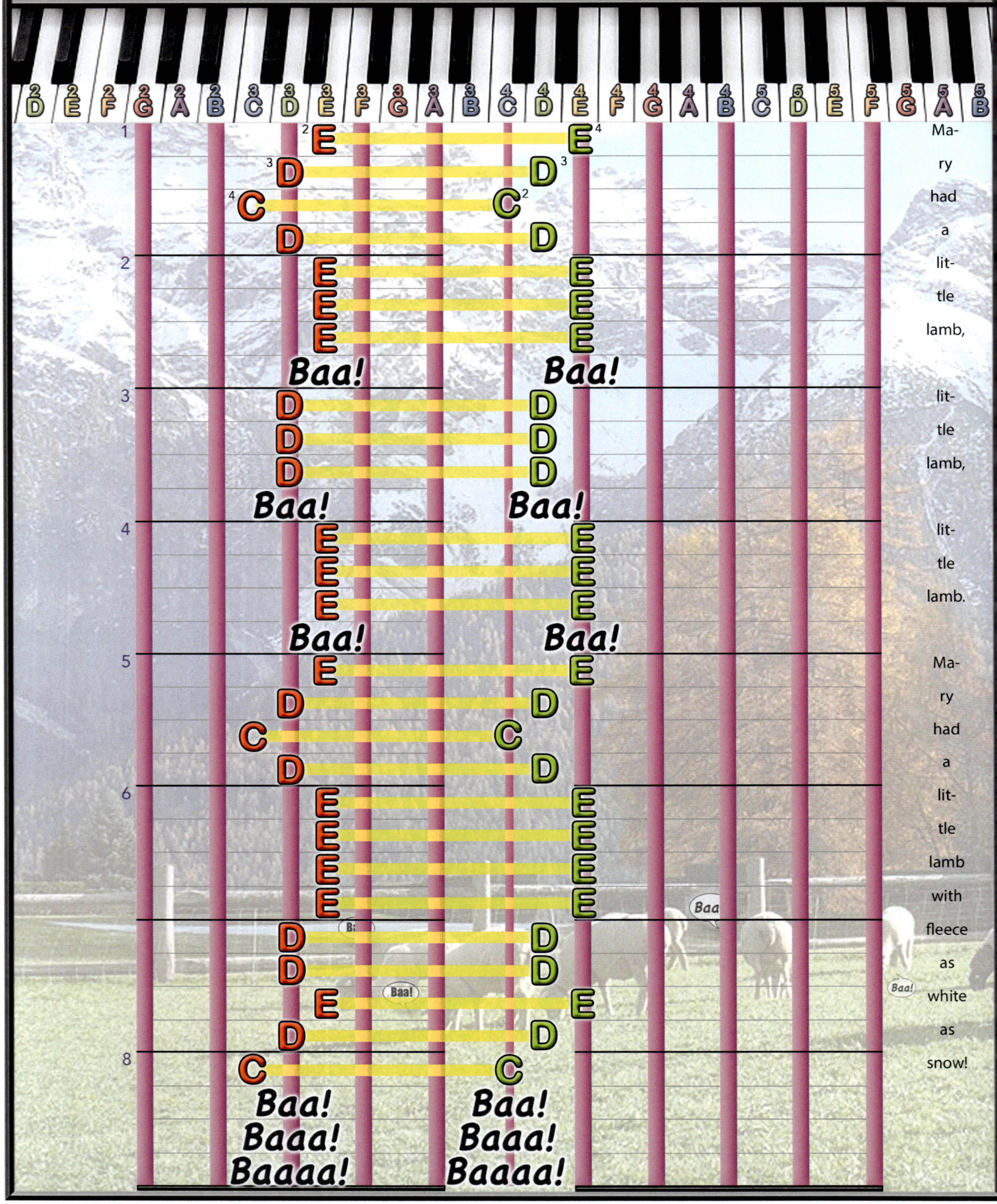

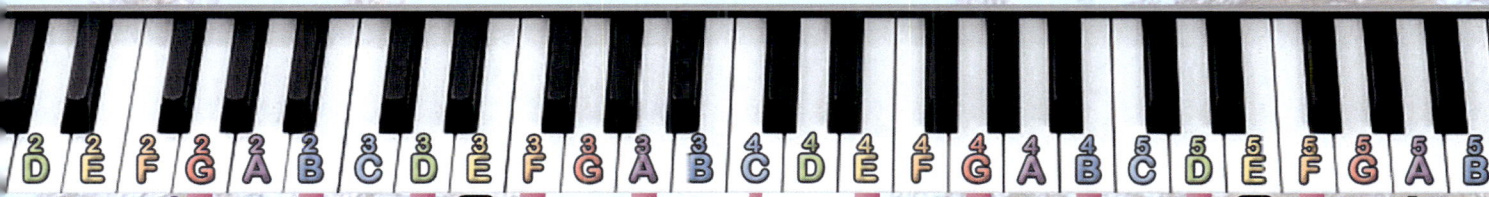

#36. Ode to Joy!
Level 11: Songs in Parallel Motion

Frue-
de
schön-
er
Göt-
ter-
fun-
ken,
Toch-
ter
aus
E-
ly-
si-
um,

Wir
Be-
tre-
ten
Feu-
er-
trun-
ken,
Himm-
li-
sche,
Dein
Hei-
lig-
tum!

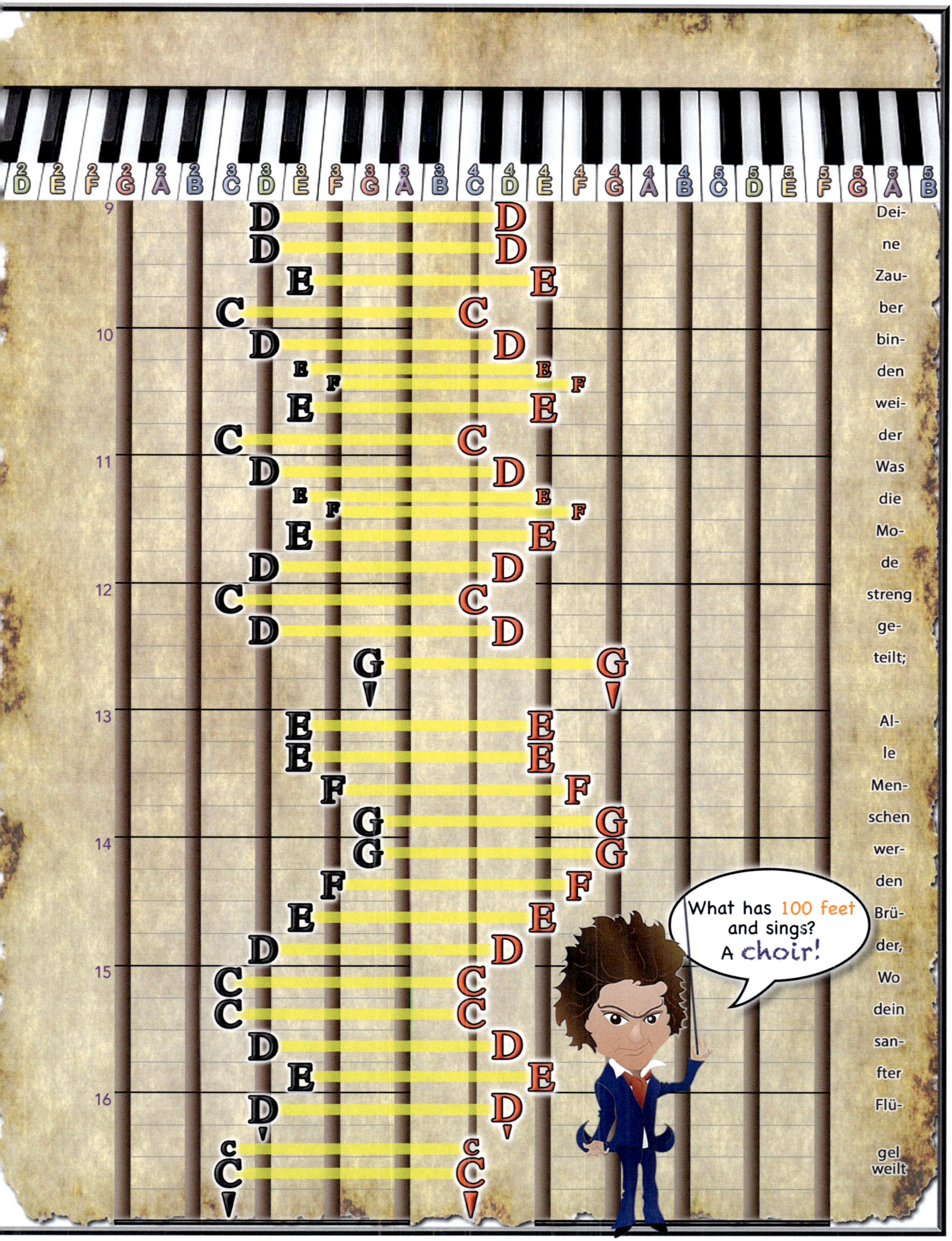
Dei- ne Zau- ber bin- den wei- der Was die Mo- de streng ge- teilt;
Al- le Men- schen wer- den Brü- der, Wo dein san- fter Flü- gel weilt
What has 100 feet and sings? A choir!

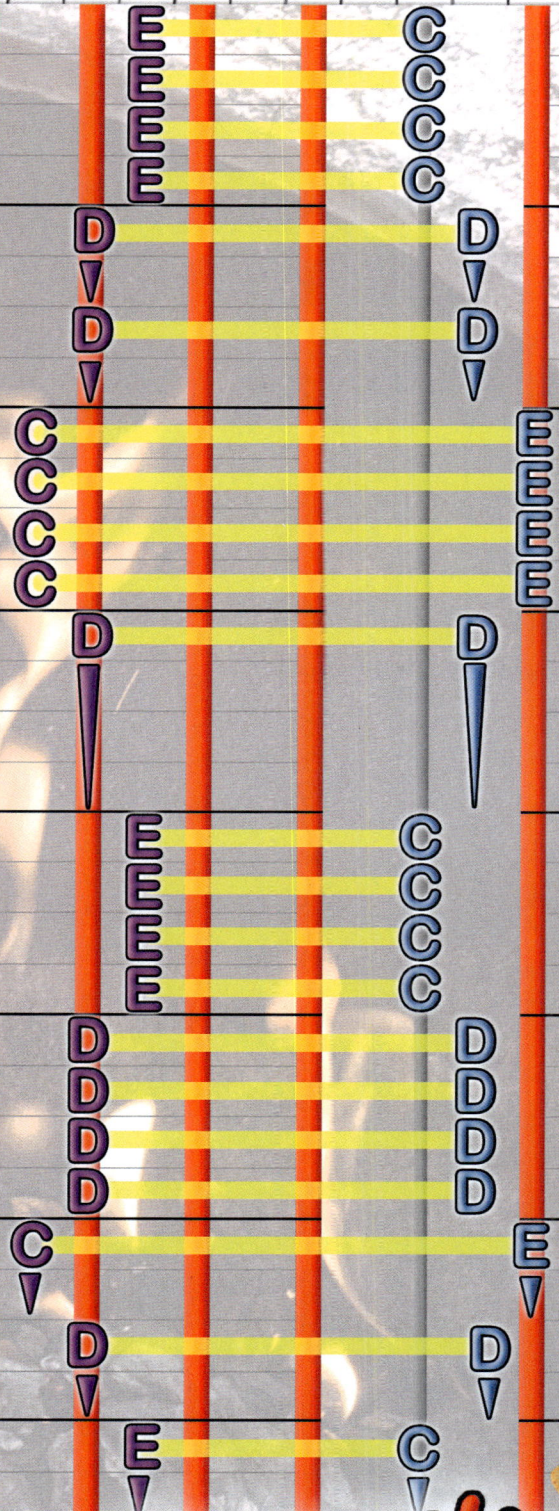

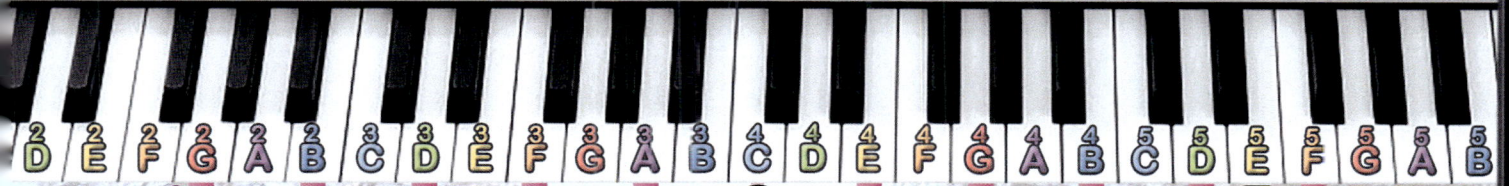

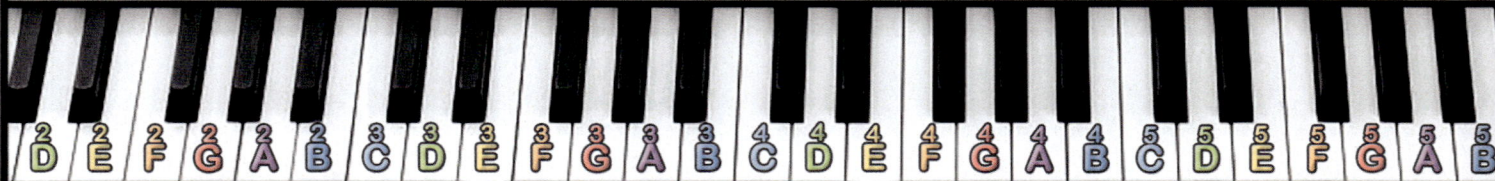

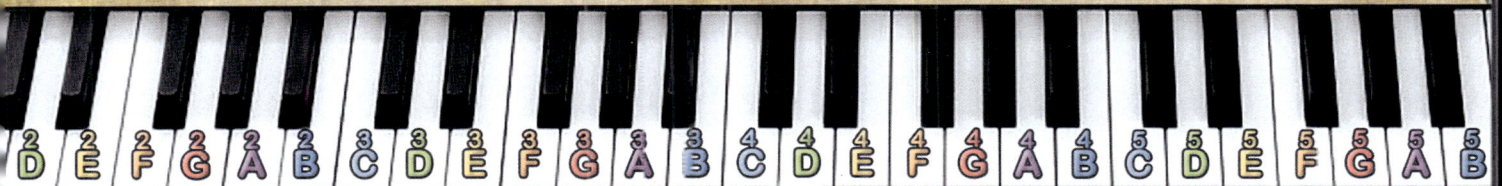

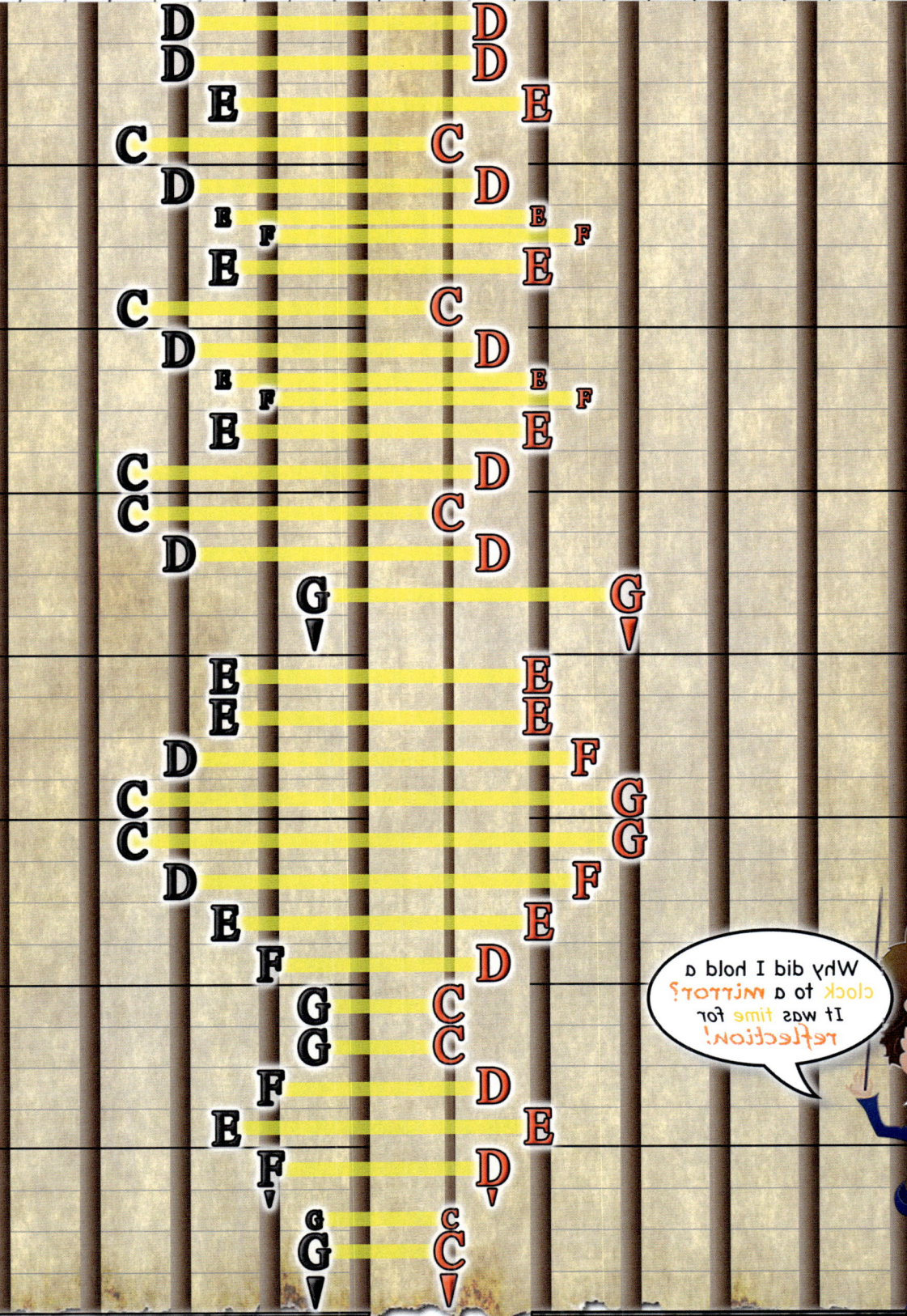

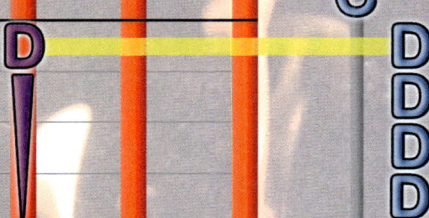

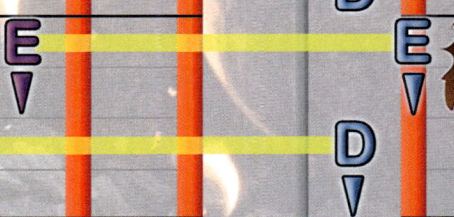

#41. SNAKE CHARMER
Level 13: Legato vs. Staccato

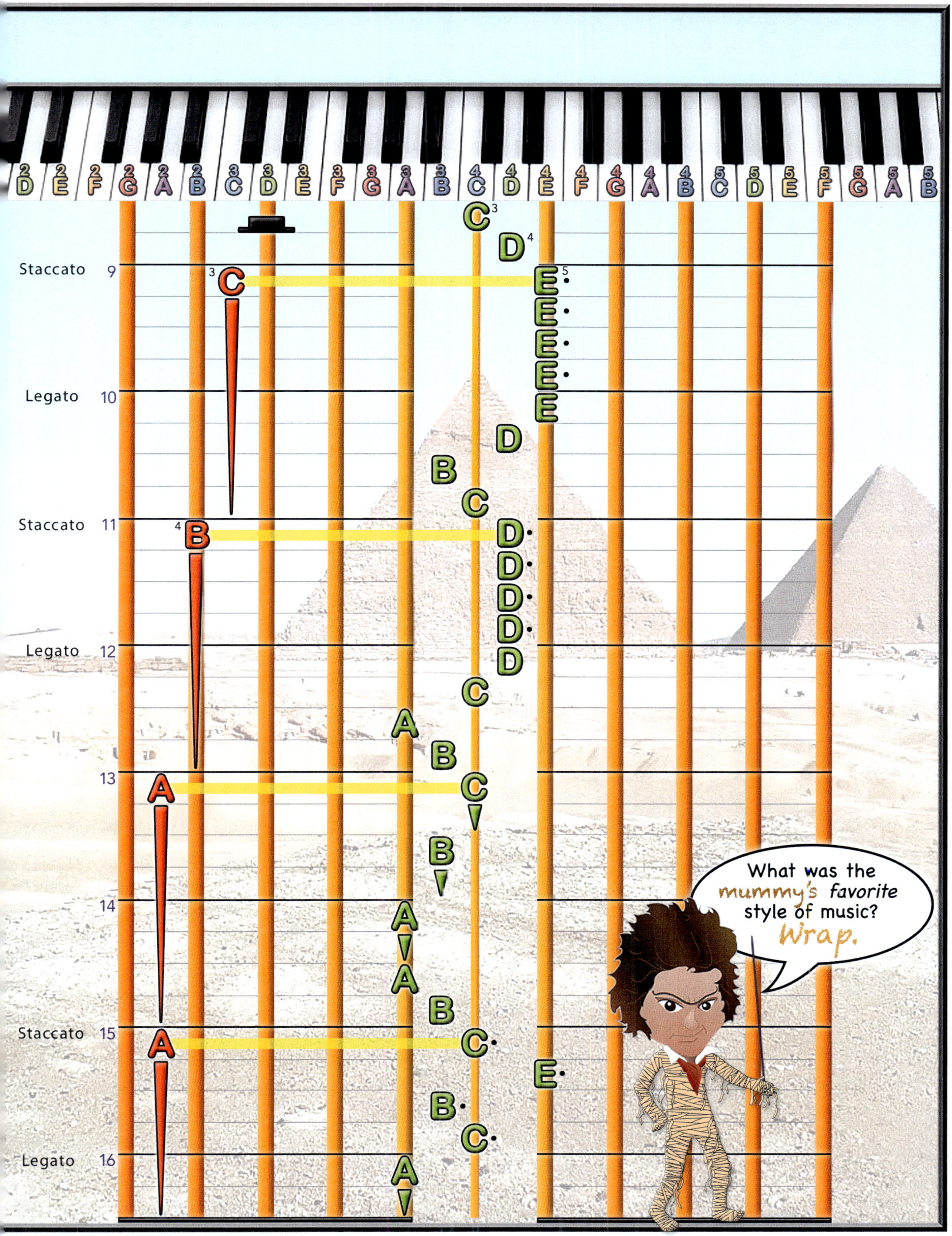

Staccato 9
Legato 10
Staccato 11
Legato 12
13
14
Staccato 15
Legato 16
What was the mummy's favorite style of music?
Wrap.

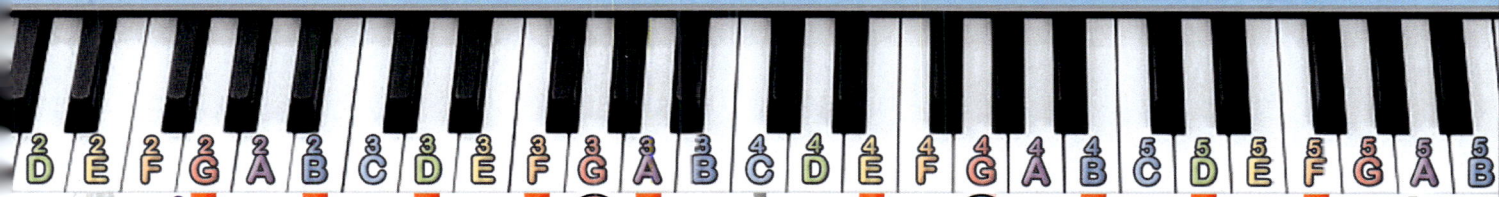

Title/Composer/Date: _____

Title/Composer/Date: _____

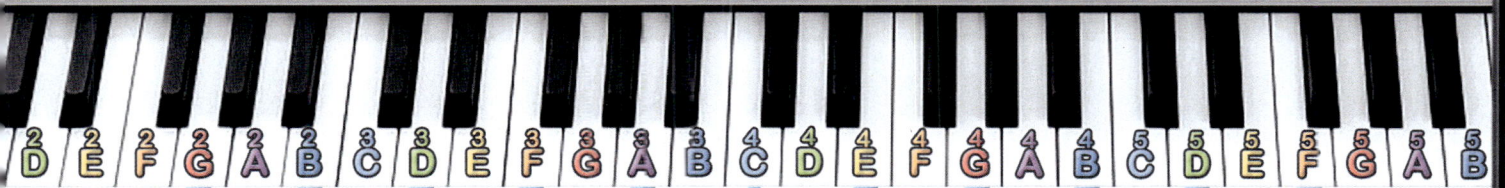

Made in the USA
Coppell, TX
09 November 2022